P9-DHA-583

A book is a present you can
open again & again!
I am happy to give this book to
the Wilder Elementary
Library in celebration of
my birthday.

Jeb Mason
April 29, 2017

Russell Wilson

By Ken Rappoport

Consultant: Barry Wilner
AP Football Writer

BEARPORT
PUBLISHING

New York, New York

WILDER ELEMENTARY LIBRARY
22130 N E. 133rd
Woodinville, WA 98072

Credits

Cover and Title Page, © Elaine Thompson/AP Images and Jim Mahoney/AP Images;
4, © Paul Jasienski/AP Images; 5, © Dan Levine/EPA/Newscom; 6, © Tacoma News Tribune/
Zumapress/Icon Sportswire; 7, © Paul Abell/AP Images; 8, © Seth Poppel/Yearbook Library;
9, © dmvphotos/Shutterstock; 10, © Seth Poppel/Yearbook Library; 11, © Sun-Sentinel/
Zuma Press/Icon Sportswire; 12, © Tony Gutierrez/AP Images; 13, © Tim Steadman/
Icon Sportswire; 14, © Robin Alam/Icon Sportswire; 15, © John Green/Cal Sport Media/
Newscom; 16, © Ted S. Warren/AP Images; 17, © Michael Conroy/AP Images; 18,
© G. Newman Lowrance/AP Images; 19, © Jon Ferrey/AP Images; 20, © Charlie Riedel/AP
Images; 21, © Paul Sancya/AP Images; 22, © Dan Levine/EPA/Newscom.

Publisher: Kenn Goin
Editor: Jessica Rudolph
Creative Director: Spencer Brinker
Photo Researcher: Chrös McDougall
Design: Emily Love

Library of Congress Cataloging-in-Publication Data

Rappoport, Ken.
  Russell Wilson / by Ken Rappoport.
      pages cm.—(Football stars up close)
  Includes bibliographical references and index.
  ISBN 978-1-62724-541-8 (library binding)—ISBN 1-62724-541-3 (library binding)
  1. Wilson, Russell, 1988—Juvenile literature. 2. Football players–United States–Biography-
Juvenile literature. 3. Quarterbacks (Football)–United States–Biography–Juvenile literature.
I. Title.
  GV939.W545R37 2015
  796.332092—dc23
  [B]
                                    2014036728

Copyright © 2015 Bearport Publishing Company, Inc. All rights reserved. No part of this
publication may be reproduced in whole or in part, stored in any retrieval system, or
transmitted in any form or by any means, electronic, mechanical, photocopying, recording,
or otherwise, without written permission from the publisher.

For more information, write to Bearport Publishing Company, Inc., 45 West 21st Street,
Suite 3B, New York, New York 10010. Printed in the United States of America.

10 9 8 7 6 5 4 3 2 1

Contents

Playoff Time

It was January 19, 2014. The Seattle Seahawks were battling the San Francisco 49ers in the **playoffs**. In his first play of the game, Seahawks **quarterback** Russell Wilson lost a **fumble**. Later, he was **sacked** four times by 49ers players. Down 17–10 in the third quarter, the Seahawks were running out of time. Would Russell be able to lead his team to victory?

Russell (far left) prepares to take a snap to start a play in the 2014 playoff game.

Russell about to throw a pass in the 2014 playoffs

The 2014 playoff game was held at the Seahawks' home stadium, CenturyLink Field.

What a Comeback!

Russell never lost his cool. He got his team close enough to the end zone to score a **field goal**. Then, in the fourth quarter, Russell launched a 35-yard (32 m) pass into the end zone. Seahawks **receiver** Jermaine Kearse made a leaping catch for a touchdown! Seattle quickly scored another field goal, and the 49ers never recovered. The Seahawks were on their way to the **Super Bowl**!

Jermaine Kearse catches the fourth-quarter touchdown.

Russell (left) and teammate
Richard Sherman celebrate
after beating the 49ers 23–17.

After the game, the Seahawks
thanked the fans in the stadium for their
constant support. Seahawks fans are
nicknamed the 12th Man. The other
11 men are the players
on the field.

Early Life

Russell was born on November 29, 1988. Sports were always important to his family. Russell loved to play baseball, basketball, and especially football. By age five, he was already playing football on a field by the local school in Richmond, Virginia. He would play quarterback while his older brother, Harrison, played receiver.

Russell (bottom) with friends in school

Russell was born in Cincinnati, Ohio, but he grew up mostly in Richmond, Virginia (shown).

When Russell was in fifth grade, he was a ball boy for his brother's high school football games. During one game, a referee yelled for a ball. He was shocked when Russell threw the ball to him at super speed.

High School Star

Russell was often told he was too short to ever play pro sports. He wasn't discouraged, though. Instead, he worked even harder. On his high school baseball team, Russell got a hit nearly every other time he batted during his senior year. On the football team, Russell could throw the ball far and on target. When no teammates were open for a pass, he charged forward with the ball.

Russell led his high school football team to three state championships.

Russell never grew taller than
5 feet 11 inches (1.8 m). Most NFL
quarterbacks are several inches taller. That's
why Russell looked up to quarterback Drew Brees.
Drew is only 6 feet (1.83 m) tall, but he led
the New Orleans Saints to a Super Bowl
title in 2010.

Drew Brees passes
the ball in the 2010
Super Bowl.

The College Game

In 2007, the Baltimore Orioles selected Russell in the **MLB draft**. He decided not to join the pro baseball team, though. He wanted to go to college and then play in the NFL. So Russell accepted a **scholarship** to North Carolina State University. There, he played on the football and baseball teams, both called the Wolfpack. On the football team, Russell set a record by throwing 379 straight pass attempts without an **interception**.

Russell chose not to play pro baseball, but he still enjoys playing the game. In 2014, he practiced with the Texas Rangers (right).

Russell was such a good student that he graduated from North Carolina State University after only three years.

Russell playing for the Wolfpack

Badger Bound

Although he had graduated, Russell was allowed to play a fourth season of college football. He decided to **transfer** to the University of Wisconsin. The school's football team, the Badgers, was in a tougher league than the Wolfpack. That meant Russell would have more skilled teammates—and tougher opponents. With the Badgers, Russell had his best passing season yet.

During his year with the Badgers, Russell threw for 33 touchdowns and just 4 interceptions.

In 2011, after Russell helped the Badgers achieve an 11–3 record, the team played in the Rose Bowl. Only college teams with winning records get invitations to bowl games.

Russell (#16) avoids getting tackled by a University of Oregon player as he runs for a touchdown in the Rose Bowl.

Draft Time

In 2012, Russell entered the NFL draft. Some teams worried he would struggle against the bigger and taller NFL players. However, the Seahawks knew he was a great leader. They respected his hard work and focus on the field. The team's coaches also knew he had a rocket for an arm and was a fast runner. Russell was thrilled when the Seahawks picked him in the draft.

Seattle coach Pete Carroll knew Russell had what it takes to succeed in the NFL.

Russell was the 75th pick in the 2012 draft. Five other quarterbacks were chosen before him.

Just before the 2012 draft, Russell showed off his throwing skills during a practice as NFL coaches watched.

Rookie Star

Russell became the **starting** quarterback during his **rookie** season with the Seahawks. Game after game, he threw passes right into receivers' arms. He rarely made mistakes. "You can never rattle him. Ever," said Seattle cornerback Richard Sherman.

In Russell's rookie season, Seattle made it to the playoffs. The next season was even better. After beating the 49ers in the 2014 playoffs, the Seahawks went to the Super Bowl.

Russell (#3) leads his teammates during a 2012 game.

Russell (#3) prepares to take a snap in a 2012 game.

In 2013, Russell broke a 75-year-old rookie record when he passed for 385 yards (352 m) in a playoff game.

Super Blowout

In the 2014 Super Bowl, the Seahawks faced the Denver Broncos. During the game, Russell threw two touchdown passes, and Seattle's defense was unstoppable. In the end, the Seahawks won the game 43–8. In his second year as a pro player, Russell had already won the NFL's biggest prize!

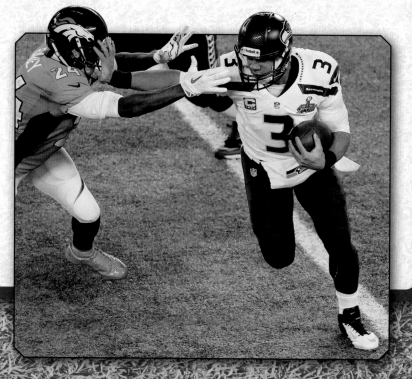

Russell (right) stiff-arms a Broncos player while running with the ball during the Super Bowl.

Russell celebrating after the Super Bowl

Super Bowl XLVIII (48) was Seattle's first Super Bowl victory.

Russell's Life and Career

★ **November 29, 1988** — Russell Wilson is born in Cincinnati, Ohio.

★ **2006** — Russell leads his high school football team to a third straight state championship.

★ **2007** — The Baltimore Orioles pick Russell in the Major League Baseball draft. He turns them down so he can go to college.

★ **2008** — Russell becomes North Carolina State's starting quarterback.

★ **2011** — Russell graduates from North Carolina State and transfers to the University of Wisconsin.

★ **2011** — Russell leads Wisconsin to an 11–3 record.

★ **2012** — The Seattle Seahawks select Russell in the NFL draft.

★ **2012** — As a rookie, Russell becomes the starting quarterback for the Seahawks and leads the team to the playoffs.

★ **2014** — Russell helps Seattle win its first Super Bowl title

Glossary

draft (DRAFT) an event in which professional sports teams take turns choosing college or high school athletes to play for them

field goal (FEELD GOHL) a score of three points made by kicking the ball through the other team's goalposts

fumble (FUHM-buhl) a ball that is dropped by the player who has it

interception (in-tur-SEP-shuhn) a pass caught by a player on the defensive team

MLB (EM ELL BEE) letters standing for *Major League Baseball*, which includes 30 teams

NFL (EN EFF ELL) letters standing for the *National Football League*, which includes 32 teams

playoffs (PLAY-awfss) games held after the end of the regular season that determine which two teams will compete in the Super Bowl

quarterback (KWOR-tur-bak) a football player who leads the offense

receiver (ri-SEE-vur) a football player who catches passes

rookie (RUK-ee) a player in his or her first season in a sport

sacked (SAKT) when a quarterback is tackled behind the line from which the play began

scholarship (SKOL-ur-ship) money given to a person so that he or she can go to college

starting (START-ing) playing at the start of a game; being the best player at a position

Super Bowl (SOO-pur BOHL) the final championship game in the NFL season

transfer (TRANSS-fur) to move from one school to another

Index

Bibliography

Babb, Kent. "Russell Wilson Has Followed an Uncommon Path." *The Washington Post* (February 2, 2014).

Official Site of the Seattle Seahawks: www.seahawks.com

Read More

Doeden, Matt. *Football's Greatest Quarterbacks (Sports Illustrated Kids)*. North Mankato, MN: Capstone (2015).

Fishman, Jon M. *Russell Wilson (Amazing Athletes)*. Minneapolis, MN: Lerner (2015).

Gitlin, Marty. *Wisconsin Badgers (Inside College Football)*. Minneapolis, MN: ABDO (2013).

Learn More Online

To learn more about Russell Wilson, visit
www.bearportpublishing.com/FootballStarsUpClose